The Death of Sunday School and the Future of Faith Formation
Discusion Guide

The Death of Sunday School and the Future of Faith Formation
Discussion Guide

Kimberly Sweeney

Courageous Faith Consulting

2017

Courageous Faith Consulting
33R Maine Avenue
Easthampton, MA 01027

www.courageousfaithconsulting.org

Ordering Information:

Special discounts are available on quantity purchases by corporations, associations, educators, and others. For details, contact the publisher at the above listed address.

Dedication

To the courageous and faithful religious professionals and lay leaders who continue to experiment boldly, dream generously, and lead with benevolence.

Thank you. For your work, your passion, and your commitment to the future of faith formation.

Contents

FROM THE AUTHOR

THIS WAS AN EXTREMELY challenging piece to write. While my experiences as a parent, religious educator, and member of the Unitarian Universalist Association's Congregational Life staff have affirmed the observations and ideas herein, it was still difficult to lay them all out on paper. At times it felt risky. Often it was overwhelming.

You may experience the tone of this writing to be bold or blunt, and that is with reason. Religious professionals have been talking about the challenges of Sunday school for close to a decade, yet talking about it and acknowledging that things need to change has not made a measurable difference. The conversations remain more or less the same year after year. Thus, it felt prudent to be as straightforward as possible.

I imagine that for some of you, reading this will affirm your own observations and experiences. Some of you may feel awash in grief and despair. Others might feel defensive. You might call to mind the mentors, parents, ministers, and teachers who spent countless hours building and supporting Sunday school programs. A few will say that your Sunday school program is thriving. I expect all of these reactions. This is holy work. Our ancestors and pioneers in religious education dedicated their lives to this call and have gifted us with an enormous history and legacy. For that we are grateful and continue to honor their contributions, selflessness, and dedication to our children and youth. A paper cannot erase that work or the impact they had. This paper was not written to diminish the work that has come before in any way.

This paper was written because while the structures of our past met the needs of families in that time and place, they are not meeting the needs of our families today. We don't build programs or develop strategies with the intention that they will live forever. We implement these programs and use these strategies for as long as they are effective and useful. While our programs and strategies should and will change over time, the purpose of our work remains the same: to bring the love and grace of Unitarian Universalism to our families' lives.

At the end of the day, I wrote this paper because the stakes felt too high to give in to my own fears. We are in rapidly evolving times, and it is mission critical that we empower one another to face this truth head on. It will be a whole lot easier if we face it together.

In faith and with tremendous appreciation,

Kim

Executive Summary

THE SUNDAY SCHOOL model of religious education has been much beloved in our Unitarian Universalist tradition. Half a century ago, and at the time of its inception, Sunday school was a significant draw for children and families and was popular in dominant culture. Over the past two decades, religious professionals and lay leaders have been questioning the effectiveness of this model. Working harder, moving things around, and investing more money in Sunday school has not increased its effectiveness. These strategies have not worked in part because we have failed to convey that the way we have always done things is no longer serving our Unitarian Universalist congregations. While we have been applying a multitude of technical fixes to this adaptive challenge, we have failed a generation of young Unitarian Universalists.

Changes in demographics, family structures, societal norms, and the role of the church in US life have evolved drastically over time. Yet the Sunday school model that came out of the twentieth century has remained relatively unchanged. Families report having to choose between spending time together or going to church and being separated. Participation in religious communities should not require families to have to sacrifice their time with one another by being shuffled in opposite directions once they enter the door. Competing priorities, generational shifts, cultural attitudes, and norms about church— coupled with local demographic shifts—have resulted in congregations in

New England having the lowest percentage of Sunday school attendance in the country.

It is past time to return to our roots by engaging, inviting, and expecting our families to worship together. It is past time to return to the ministry of preparing parents and caregivers to be the primary religious educators for their children. It is past time to bury Sunday school, a model that has not been adapted to contemporary times. The future of faith formation resides in family ministry.

Ending Sunday school is not tantamount to ending faith formation. To the contrary, faith formation is a foundational ethos of our Unitarian Universalist ministries. Paying attention to the shifting needs of our families and children, releasing ourselves from the structures of our past, and boldly experimenting to contribute to the evolution of faith formation may just be the spiritual task of our time. The future of Unitarian Universalist faith formation in New England depends on it.

THE DEATH OF SUNDAY SCHOOL

The Death of Sunday School

THE SUNDAY SCHOOL model of religious education died in New England two decades ago. Many leaders had a sense that its death was coming, but the passing was subtle and While we have been taking our time moving in out of the stages of grief, sometimes lingering in or returning to denial, we have failed a generation of young Unitarian Universalists. We have been unable to part ways with Sunday school and have done everything we could think of to resuscitate it, to the detriment of our youth and their families. We have a responsibility to bury Sunday school and move forward before we lose another generation. It is imperative to the future of our faith.

For the majority of the history of religion in the United States, faith formation has occurred outside of a classroom. Several centuries ago, when the nation housed far less religious diversity, children were most often raised in the shared faith tradition of their family. Families recognized the Sabbath or Shabbat together. "Seventeenth-century New England Puritans took the Sabbath very seriously, enacting harsh measures, known as Blue Laws, to punish the impious. Starting in the mid-1600s, any Sunday activity that took away from worship—shopping, laundry, consumption of alcohol, "unseemly" walking—was strictly forbidden".[1] Aspects of these Blue Laws remained in effect for centuries, leaving household responsibilities and worship as the only options for Sunday activities. Families prayed together, celebrated the traditions of their faith together, and worshipped together. This was faith formation. For Indigenous peoples, faith formation was interwoven and imbued in all aspects of living. Sunday school did not exist. In fact, the earliest public schools in the United States were not academi-

13

cally focused, but instead taught morality and virtues, focusing on family, religion, and community. It wasn't until the mid–nineteenth century that public education shifted its focus to academics, and even then classes were mostly multi-aged.

The American Unitarian Association embraced graded curriculum—lessons designed for different age levels, a progressive innovation—in 1909 with its "Beacon Series." But by the 1930s, Unitarianism was in crisis. Membership had dropped to 50,228 in 1935. The *Christian Register* reported widespread dissatisfaction with Unitarian Sunday school programs in 1930.[2]

Educational theorists (e.g., Dewey, Piaget, and Erikson) and educational reform were responsible for the current academically focused, age-segregated model of public education in the United States.

Religious Education Class 1945-46

It wasn't until the 1940s and 1950s that the Sunday school model we recognize today came to life. Church and religion still played a significant role in US culture. Sunday school mimicked the structure of public schools, providing age-segregated classes for children to receive religious instruction and lessons. Weekly attendance was the norm, and perfect attendance awards were not uncommon. In New England, these programs were often run by the minister's spouse or by another parent in the congregation. It was decades before program administrators (or Directors of Religious Education) were compensated for their work.

The 1960s and 1970s ushered in an anti-establishment culture with Baby Boomers rebelling against institutions, including church.

> *We rebelled by dropping out: 2/3rds of my generation dropped out of church. In the late 1970's/early 1980's, innovative pastors and congregations of all sizes and denominations looked for ways to draw Boomers back to church. They began to create worship experiences based on the unique "personality" of the Boomer generation. These churches went "contemporary," "seeker," and/or "seeker-friendly." Because these were the primary parenting years for Boomers, these congregations recognized the need to not only provide Boomer-friendly worship experiences for adults, but the need to create dynamic experiences for their children as well, knowing that if the kids wanted to come back, the parents were more likely to come back.[3]*

Thus began the shift from families worshipping together to creative and attractive Sunday school programs for kids, offered at the same time as the worship service. Suddenly, in Unitarian Universalist spaces, children and adults were having drastically different Sunday morning experiences in isolation from each other. These programs eventually moved to a cooperative model where parents volunteered to run the Sunday school program and teach the classes as well. Some churches would exclude children from the worship experience, expecting Sunday school to engage them and meet their needs until such time as they became recognized as adults. Many still do.

The pendulum swung from one direction where congregations gathered as a single body (mixing), to the other direction where people were gathering by age or cohort (huddling). The long-term and unintended consequence of this strategy was a generation of young people who had no connection to their faith or congregation outside of Sunday school. The implicit message of this divergent approach was that what happened in the sanctuary was for adults; it was framed as being boring and unappealing for children. Young people spent their childhood and adolescence segregated from the adult congregation. In our

15

Unitarian Universalist tradition, bridging out of the youth ministry program essentially meant bridging out of the church. The only connection of youth to the church was through their peers, who were also moving on.

Changes in demographics, family structures, societal norms, and the role of the church in dominant white US culture have evolved drastically over time.[4] Yet the Sunday school model that came out of the twentieth century has remained relatively unchanged.

> *For the past century Christian churches have structured their faith formation programs for children around a classroom model. This approach brings together teachers and children for regular, planned teaching and learning, in settings where significant relationships take shape. Many churches still structure their children's program around the "traditional" classroom model, which looks and feels the same as it did decades ago. The books and materials have been updated, but the basic model remains. This model served churches in previous generations, but changes in families, society, and churches have accentuated its limitations.[5]*

When Baby Boomers were in their prime parenting years, the current structure of age-segregated Sunday school classes was born. Finding volunteers wasn't much of a challenge for a generation of roughly eighty million at a time when many two-parent households had only one parent working outside the home. But today's generation of parents, Generation X, is roughly half the size of the Baby Boomer generation, with intense expectations and requirements for volunteerism. The number of volunteers needed to staff these programs has not changed, but the number of adults in this generation has decreased by 50 percent.[6] Add in the decrease of religious identity in each successive generation, changes in family structure, the economic reality that necessitates more parents working outside the home, and

16

(...this is now)

- **Attendance is down in Sunday school**

- **Children attend sporadically**

- **Volunteer teachers are hard to find**

- **Families are choosing between spending time together on Sundays or being separated at church**

the culture of intense over-scheduling affecting people of all ages in our society, and there just isn't the capacity to replace the Baby Boomer volunteer base.

Religious educators report, " Teacher recruitment time is one of the most demoralizing times of my job for me," and "I need teachers and childcare providers. Thus far, all recruiting has been futile, even for paid positions." This structure essentially sets up our religious educators for failure.

It has long been recognized that parents and families play a significant and vital role in the faith development of children and youth. Sociological and demographic changes have made a substantial impact on twenty-first-century family structures and even the numerous ways the concept of family is named or defined. Families are often pulled in a variety of directions and experience no shortage of competition for their time. For many families, Sunday is often the only time of the week when they are all at home at the same time.

Families report having to choose between spending time together or going to church and being separated. Participation in religious communities should not require families to have to sacrifice their time with one another by being shuffled in opposite directions once they enter the door.

These observations and cultural realities explain, in part, religious educators reporting a sharp decline in Sunday school attendance for the past many years. Competing priorities, generational shifts, and cultural attitudes and norms about church, coupled with local demo-

17

> *Unfortunately many congregations have contributed to the situation by over- emphasizing age-segregated programming, which further divides families, and over-programming family members. Oftentimes there is little to no programming that engages the entire family as a family, or that empowers and equips parents for their task as the primary religious teachers of their children and teens. Sadly, many churches blame parents for the situation or have given up on families, "because they don't come to Sunday worship or the programs we offer, so why bother."[7]*

graphic shifts, have led to congregations in New England having the lowest percentage of Sunday school attendance in the country.[8]

New England has seen a sharp increase in the turnover of UU Directors of Religious Education in the past five years, an increase in positions that go unfilled, and a decrease in the number of applicants overall. At the time of this writing, New England UU congregations were experiencing twenty-five staff transitions in religious education. By the end of May 2017, only six of those positions had been filled, four of which were filled by applicants new to the field. The remaining nineteen positions range from full time to three hours a week, and have received minimal interest from applicants regardless of their background or training. The average number of staff transitions for religious educators in New England was thirty-three annually from 2015 to 2017. Newer religious educators are less inclined to apply for positions steeped in the traditional Sunday school model. Even with the offer of fair compensation and benefits, religious educators are increasingly wary of maintaining declining religious education programs.

It bears noting that there is no prescribed pathway to a career as a Unitarian Universalist religious educator. Our religious educators are hired from a wide and varied spectrum of experiences, education, and backgrounds. Some have previously served as volunteers in religious education, while others come with backgrounds in education, art, music, social work, and many other fields. Unlike ordained clergy who have attended seminary, there is no single training, experience, or course that our religious educators can be expected to have completed before coming to this work. Their professional development often happens while they are serving, not during their preparation for the work, and the education they receive varies greatly depending on the needs, interests, and financial commitment of the congregation. Religious educators wishing to be credentialed through the Unitarian Universalist Association are only able to begin the process after they have been in the work for some time.

In New England, the majority of religious educator positions are half-time or less, with many congregations increasingly reducing the hours of these positions. Quarter-time positions maintain the disconnection between children and the rest of the congregation because there is simply no staff time to align the religious education program with the rest of the church. In effect, the congregation is paying a person to keep young people busy and separate from the rest of the congregation.

In actuality, Generation X is the most highly educated generation, graduated from school with the highest rate of student debt, and is the first generation in modern US history that will earn less than their parents. Part-time, low-paying or stipend positions without benefits that require no educational background are not attractive, sustainable, or realistic for this generation. Unitarian Universalism is stuck between a model that worked successfully two generations ago and a model that we have yet to fully imagine or articulate. We have inherited a Sunday school model that depends on unpaid or underpaid leadership, despite decades of tremendous dedication and sacrifice. We are in a time when that is simply not an option for our current workforce.

An interfaith poll of US congregations found that only 16 percent of all Sunday school programs are run by religious educators. Over 70 percent of these programs are managed by clergy or volunteers.[9] With the majority of Sunday school programs being organized peripherally by clergy or by impassioned and untrained lay volunteers, it is no wonder that we continue to maintain this structure. We haven't had the time or capacity to make way for something new. The culture

19

shift required to be the relevant faith communities our children and families need today is considerable.

There are six key facts that feel particularly relevant to this conversation of how the Unitarian Universalist model of religious education must change, and why culture shift is called for instead of more superficial solutions.

1. As stewards of our Unitarian Universalist faith, it is our responsibility to adapt our approaches to faith formation to these contemporary times.

New England is seeing significant demographic shifts as the Baby Boomer generation continues to age. Connecticut, Maine, New Hampshire, Rhode Island, and Vermont are among the nine states in the country with the oldest populations, with New Hampshire, Maine, and Vermont being the top three.

By 2020, the US Census predicts that 20 percent of New Hampshire's 1.3 million residents will be sixty-five or older, up from 13.5 percent in 2010.[10] Public school enrollment in New Hampshire has fallen more than 10 percent over the past decade, and population projections forecast that decline to continue through the coming decade. In Vermont, the number of births has been on a steady decline for the past 15 years, a major factor contributing to Vermont's population stagnation and to the declining number of students in its schools. A 2016 headline read, "Number of VT Births Lowest since before Civil War."[11]

The result of these trends is that there are fewer children and youth living in New England than in previous generations.[12] For example, a UU congregation in Maine offers a Sunday morning religious education program for infants through high school–age youth, yet the only public school in town has only between three and eight students enrolled at each grade level. Dozens of other New England congregations frequently report needing to combine classes or operate with a one-room-schoolhouse model on Sunday mornings due to minimal attendance numbers.

20

Elders will make up the overwhelming majority of the membership of UU churches for decades to come, and there is no reason to believe that attendance numbers for children and youth in Sunday school programs will rise. Sunday school in New England is dead. We don't have the children, the time, the volunteers, or the staff to maintain this outdated structure of faith formation.[13]

Religious leaders have been talking about these demographic shifts for two decades. John Roberto got religious professionals talking about it in 2010 with the research in his book, *Faith Formation 2020.*[14] Despite much talking, and learning, and tweaking programs, for the most part the systems and structures remain unchanged.

Even at the end of her long career, revolutionary Unitarian religious educator Sophia Lyon Fahs continued to put forth questions about the nature of religious truths and the adequacy of church school structures in passing on religion.[15] For nearly a decade, religious professionals and lay leaders alike have been asking questions too, such as:"

How can we attract more children and families to our church?

What can we do in religious education to make kids want to come on Sunday?

How can we invite more people to volunteer to staff the religious education program?

Where can we find a religious educator who can bring our program back to life?

Despite the demographic shifts discussed above, many congregations throughout New England feel that they are not "doing church right" without a religious education program, even in towns where there are hardly any children.

2. Finding a different religious educator is not the key.

The most skilled, talented, and experienced religious educators out there are as unable to change demographic shifts as anyone else. Hiring a religious educator to maintain or reinvigorate a religious education program using an outdated structure will not yield different results. Ask yourself, "If the structure of the program remains roughly unchanged, and none of the religious educators in the past ten years have been able to 'reinvigorate' the program, might it be possible that the structure is no longer working?"

3. Increasing staffing to minister to specific subsets of young people maintains age segregation.

Part-time positions that minister to five or ten kids each Sunday implicitly suggest that a congregation would prefer to pay someone to manage, entertain, or teach its children than engage in religious community with them.

4. As Baby Boomers move into retirement and Gen X moves into leadership and lay positions, the size of the volunteer pool is cut nearly in half.

Combine the smaller volunteer pool with adults who want to be in worship and families that want to stay together on Sunday morning, and there simply are not enough adults left to staff the volunteer-heavy Sunday school model of yesterday.

5. A curriculum will not save the day.

There is no curriculum out there that will bring a religious education program back to the levels of participation seen twenty or thirty years ago. There is no curriculum waiting to be written that will do that either. Curriculum is not the issue. A curriculum does not determine whether or not a family will participate on Sunday morning.

6. Adults need just as much faith formation as children and youth.

22

Roughly 88 percent of adult members come to Unitarian Universalism from other faith traditions or from no tradition at all.[16] The lack of faith development for UU adults is a serious problem, resulting in a high percentage of adults with a tenuous connection to or understanding of Unitarian Universalism. Parents and other adults within a congregation cannot be the guides our children need until they have developed their own spiritual capacity.

Dr. Diana Butler Bass, author, speaker, and independent scholar specializing in US religion and culture, relates this story:

A few years ago, I attended a rapidly growing congregation in California. Most of the newcomers fit one of two categories. They were either returning baby- boomers or spiritual seekers. Most returnees had grown up in a mainline tradition but quit church in their teens or early twenties. They had lots of emotional and spiritual baggage regarding the Bible, theology, and Christian tradition. Many of the seekers, often Gen Xers, had rarely been inside a church.

Those of us in congregational leadership quickly realized that we had a set of problems. How to honor the life experience and practical wisdom of the returnees while helping them to theological maturity? And how, at the same time, to introduce unchurched people to the fullness of life in [religious] community?

Our problem was not evangelism. People were coming to the church. Our problem was adult education.

And, still worse news: no single curriculum or program could help us. We needed to fashion an introduction to church that worked in our setting. Adult formation would be a process, not a program. We needed to understand our own identity and communicate our vision of faith and vocation to the new members.[17]

Herein lies the opportunity to consider what Unitarian Universalist congregations can contribute to the evolution of faith formation in a way that is relevant spiritually and contextually and is mindful of the contemporary realities of the day. Congregations can meet the needs of twenty-first-century families—we have evidence that this is true.

It is past time to return to our roots of engaging, inviting, and expecting our families to worship together. It is past time to return to the ministry of preparing parents and caregivers to be the primary religious educators for their children. It is past time to bury Sunday school, a model that has not been adapted to contemporary times.

THE FUTURE OF FAITH FORMATION

The Future of Faith Formation

TODAY'S REFORMATION calls for the centering of faith formation in the mission of our communities of faith. The reformation called for within Unitarian Universalism asks religious educators to lead in a new way. Religious educators are being invited to engage the entire congregation in faith formation, bringing certitude to the words of UU leader Connie Goodbread, " Faith development is all we do. Unitarian Universalism is the faith we teach. The congregation is the curriculum."

Today's reformation calls for the de-centering of dominant ways of doing things and dominant experiences of the world. It calls for the de-centering of the older adult experience, the de-centering of whiteness, the de-centering of upper-class norms, all in service of our vision for a multicultural, multiracial and multigenerational Unitarian Universalism. As the Rev. Dr. Mark Morrison-Reed has put it, we are moved to do this because we "see the richness in human diversity and [are] excited by its possibility." Given the cultural context in which we

26

now find ourselves, this is where Unitarian Universalism's deepest theological principles and religious values draw us. Religious liberalism has always been marked by its ability to engage and respond to the circumstances of its own time and place. This is what has kept our UU theology intellectually credible and socially relevant. If we fail to respond to our new multicultural reality—if we choose to stand rather than to move—we will not only fail to honor this core principle of liberal theology, we also will simply become irrelevant.[18]

The future of faith formation resides in family ministry. The concept of family ministry isn't new. Our evolving definitions of family may change, but the call to support faith formation at both church and home remains true. Reggie Joiner, founder and president of the reThink Group, frames it this way:

> *The church realizes it can't be effective alone and needs the home. As family ministry expands, it's also evolving. Just being family-friendly no longer counts. The old approach of keeping people of all ages busy with lots of family-specific programming is missing the mark. All the "random acts of ministry" that churches line up for families overload church and family schedules, ultimately "competing with the very families you're trying to help."*[19]

Churches have been focused on resourcing faith formation that happens within their walls, and have failed to focus adequate time, attention, and resources to equip families to do the work of faith formation at home. Being contemporarily relevant will challenge us to move away from an educational and entertaining model of religious education in service of intentionally working to meet the faith formation needs of families today.

There are many ways in which congregations can partner with parents and caregivers to bring faith formation out of the church and

27

into the home. One effort to bridge the gap between Sunday school and home is the "taking it home" segment of Tapestry of Faith curricula.[20] While the goal was commendable, most of those "taking it home" sheets are left behind during coffee hour or crumpled up in the back seat of the car on the drive home (and if you didn't attend the religious education class on Sunday, you didn't receive the handout).

A more inspiring effort was "Full Week Faith," an approach offered by Karen Bellavance- Grace that served as a bridge between church and home.[21] Full Week Faith tried to redefine faith formation as something we do in more than just one hour a week. Knowing that we are in the middle of a seismic shift in the landscape of religious life, it offered a transitional model for forming faith without certainty of what the new paradigm would be, citing family ministry as one of its core pillars.

Family ministry aims to support families of all configurations by modeling how to bring our faith home. Often times, Unitarian Universalists simply need to be reminded or shown that there are ways to do just that. From stories and songs to spiritual practices and social justice opportunities, from ethical eating and voting as a person of faith to celebrating Lent or Advent in affirming ways, there are numerous ways in which to model bringing our faith out of the sanctuary and into our lives.

Mike Clear, family life pastor at Discovery Church in Simi Valley, California, reinforces the importance of intentionality. "Family ministry needs to be about churches intentionally influencing parents to be the spiritual leader for their kids," he says. A child might attend church some fifty hours per year, but a parent or caregiver has more like three thousand hours per year "to impact the heart of their child"—an influence that is lifelong. "As good as we might think we are as a church and as electrifying and relevant as our ministries might be, we still don't have the potential to influence children the way parents do," Clear says.[22]

The purpose of faith formation programs is to bring the love and grace of Unitarian Universalism to our families' lives. A compelling and supported path to disciplined spiritual maturity is central to congregational life. While the majority of UU congregations' focus has been on providing faith formation opportunities for children and youth, most parents still expect congregational life to support them in forming their children into spiritual beings. How can this happen if the parent or caregiver is not also engaging in faith formation? Faith formation is a lifelong process. If we are to bring the love and grace of this faith to our families' lives, we must intentionally support the faith formation of both our children and our adults.

Considering the pendulum swung from mixing to huddling, it's now time to land somewhere in between, offering opportunities for people of all ages to be in community together (mixing), as well as opportunities to gather with peers in similar ages or stages of life (huddling). Intentional family ministry provides adults with opportunities to dig deeper into their own beliefs, strengthening their ability to discuss the values and history of Unitarian Universalism with their children. Parents and caregivers have space to talk about the spiritual aspects of parenting, or learn how to support their teenagers as they go through Our Whole Lives. With intentional family ministry, faith formation is no longer seen as just for children. In fact, it is structured in a way that encourages participation from the entire congregation.

Some congregations offer just such opportunities each Sunday after a traditional worship service in their second-hour religious education program, including the UU Church of Chattanooga, Tennessee; the UU Congregation of Duluth, Minnesota; Emerson UU Chapel in the greater St. Louis, Missouri, area; the UU Church of Annapolis, Maryland; and the UU Church of Ogden. Some of these opportunities are age-specific (e.g., Our Whole Lives, Spirit Play, Tapestry of Faith) and some are specific to life stages (e.g., parenting, emerging adults, retirement) or interests (e.g., small group ministry, particular spiritual practices). Family ministry varies greatly depending on the specific needs of any congregation.

Intentional family ministry welcomes the whole congregation to worship together on Sunday morning. Gone are the days of families going in opposite directions upon arriving at church, under this model. Children have the opportunity to witness and be a part of the traditions of worship. Congregations can come together as a singular community for that one hour each week, instead of being fragmented by worship, children's classes, and youth group. While whole-congregation worship may be countercultural within Unitarian Universalism today, it is much more welcoming and conscious of the beloved community we aim to be.

For most UU congregations, moving to whole congregation worship would be a substantial shift. In many of our congregations there might be some reluctance or anxiety in even considering it. Unitarian Universalism is one of the few denominations in the United States that assumes that children cannot and should not be in weekly worship with adults for an hour. The Unitarian Universalist Association's 2005 Commission on Appraisal report found that "the way UUs raise our children seems to prepare them for something completely different than what Unitarian Universalism actually offers. This suggests that UUs should change one or the other (or both)."[23]

Without experiencing worship with the whole congregation, UU children and youth cannot learn how to be in a sanctuary, let alone benefit from the spiritual practice of congregational worship. They cannot see adults modeling moments of silence or stewardship, caring deeply for one another with expressions of joy and sorrow, singing the songs of our faith, or sharing in the ministry of worship.

If the above alone is not enough, here are twelve more reasons to welcome children in church:[24]

1. Children are people too: When we welcome kids in church, we acknowledge that they are important humans and community members in the present, not just in the future.

2. A kid-friendly church is a parent-friendly church: When we welcome children, we are making their caregivers feel welcome too.

3. Children learn by participating: When we welcome kids, we invite them to experience the sacred in community with adults.

4. Kids can handle sermons: When we involve children in church, we expose them to deep, important ideas.

30

5. It's good for everyone: When we include kids in church, we all get to practice being more generous with each other.

6. It makes services better: When we plan for children to be involved, we plan better, richer services.

7. Kids have lots to offer: When we welcome children, they are able to contribute their time and skills.

8. It makes us stronger: When we welcome kids in church, we strengthen relationships across generations.

9. It can improve preaching: When we include children in church, our preachers are prompted to do a better job for everyone and make sermons more accessible to all.

10. Adults don't miss out: When kids are part of the church service, adults don't have to choose between worshipping and leading or attending kids' programs.

11. It helps young people bridge the gap: When we include people in services from a young age, they have a less jolting transition in adolescence.

12. It models welcome: When we welcome kids in church, we demonstrate how welcome everyone is.

Research shows that "involvement in all-church worship during high school is more consistently linked with mature faith in both high school and college than any other form of church participation."[25] What is the best way to prepare high school–aged youth for attending worship? Establishing it as a practice in childhood.

Knowing and being known by people of all generations needs to be an expectation of congregational life. There is clear evidence that young people benefit from multiple, sustained relationships outside of their immediate family. To grow up healthy, our youth need to be supported and known by at least five adults in addition to their

31

parents or caregivers who are willing to invest time with them person-
ally and spiritually.[26] Very often Unitarian Universalist congregants
report wanting more multigenerational experiences, yet they aren't
being given such opportunities with the young people in our congregations. "Effective religious socialization comes about through em-
bedded practices; that is, through specific, deliberate religious activities that are firmly intertwined with the daily habits of family
routines . . . and of being part of a community."[27]

We are more age-segregated as a society now than perhaps
ever before. Younger generations of adults are transient and mobile.
Older generations have moved out of their neighborhoods, sometimes
into retirement communities or assisted living facilities, which are often not in the same town or state as their children or families. Children are further segregated in schools, with typically only a few grades
housed within the same building. We need multigenerational connections, but mainstream culture conspires to keep the generations apart
and isolate them from each other. Our congregations are one of the
last places in our society where people of all ages can come together.

What Have We Learned?

RELIGIOUS EDUCATORS, ministers, and lay leaders have been talking in varying degrees about the need for the reformation of religious education programs and faith formation practices for decades. Collegial conversations, common reads, and shared trainings alone have not been effective strategies for ushering in change of this magnitude. Numerous technical approaches have been initiated to no avail.

We have learned that the future of faith formation requires adaptive leadership. It also requires the attention and engagement of the congregation as a whole. Culture shift, embracing new norms, and bold experimentation is too much for a single person to establish alone. Unitarian Universalists have done this work before. Those who came before us saw the need to attend to the religious education of children in ways they had never seen before. Unitarian Universalists can do this work again.

We have learned of the tremendous impact collaborative shared ministry can have when ministers and religious educators are able to work together in service of one whole congregation. The most vital and thriving congregations practice covenantal shared ministry among their staff and lay leaders. Perhaps the 2013 Excellence in Shared Ministry report said it best:

33

The best we can hope for our religion is that the future we co-create is rooted in our heretical heritage. We stand on the shoulders of people who, against mandates of their day, promoted counter-cultural ideas. "Freedom, reason, and tolerance," resounded from their lips and their living, though their world was steeped in proscription and intolerance. Still, we must acknowledge that while this is our foundation, it is not our current battle. Tolerance and freedom are touted widely in popular culture. Quests of the individual (See me. Accept me. Make room for me.) fail to address the desperate isolation in which we all live.

Our faith currently offers a vital alternative. Without the dictates of dogma, we are freed to create the substantive covenantal communities in which people can recover a sense of connection to self, others and spirit. Ours is the religion that binds us first to the other and in doing so to all that is holy or life itself. We can hold each other. We can love each other because of who we are not in spite of who we are. We can love each other into being more.

That lofty, but attainable goal, requires living into reality the notion that our religion is at its core about transformation. Engagement with this faith, true engagement, means that we will be changed by it. Thus, our religious professionals are agents of transformation. As such, we are called upon to be modelers and guides of the spirits, rather than technicians of separate aspects of our religion. We are called to lead and to do so in relationship. We are called to[28] *model covenantal living and shared empowerment.*

In her book *Salsa, Soul, and Spirit*, Juana Bordas writes about how incorporating leadership models of communities of color can strengthen the whole: "Leaders in communities of color . . . are the link between the past, present, and future. They promote a sense of continuity and wholeness."[29] The Honorable Anna Escobedo Cabral, former Treasurer of the United States, observes:

> *Leaders in our community have a really good sense of the past and how it relates to the present. However, they know that in the end, they have to address the challenges the community is facing today, and be concerned with the impact on the future. Our past guides us. It is important to know the struggles our community has faced, but we cannot live in the past. The challenge is to make sure the community is evolving and creating a better future.*[30]

We know that leaders must engage the whole of our communities if we are to evolve. What leaders invite people to talk, think, and pray about determines the path they will follow into the future. Leaders have the power of agenda: determining what a congregation should focus on by devoting time and attention to that conversation.

In his book *Doing the Math of Mission*, Gil Rendle describes three types of leadership conversations: maintenance, preferential, and missional.[31]

Congregations engaging in maintenance conversations will find themselves focused on preserving who they are and what they usually do. This might show up as maintaining a declining Sunday school program for those who show up.

35

Congregations engaging in preferential conversations will find themselves focused on satisfying the people who are already in the congregation. They will also be searching for ways to keep people happy and unchanged. This might look like a Sunday school model that bases their programming on what people who show up say they want. For example, learning about world religions, more time spent outside, or building a house out of cardboard like we did with the haunted house curricula forty-two years ago! Trying to keep each person happy is never possible, and negates the possibility of planning strategically.

Congregations able to have missional conversations will focus on purpose and the possibility of the future. Missional conversations where people truly say "yes!" create the possibility for the evolution of a church's relevance, and—in this case—its approach to faith formation.

Unitarian Universalist congregations that have had these missional conversations and have moved beyond the Sunday school model have offered these pieces of advice:

1. Communicate early, often, and in every conceivable way. Preach from the pulpit, include articles in the newsletter, host conversations. People need to feel heard. It can be important to have intentional conversations with stakeholders, especially those you anticipate will be upset or most resistant.

2. Remember: people aren't afraid of change; they are afraid of loss. There may be hesitation or resistance in releasing ourselves from the current model, especially if it is the model we grew up with, taught in, volunteered for, or watched children be a part of. This may be the only model the majority of a congregation has ever been exposed to or can imagine. Many congregations have experienced a sense of shame or failure when their Sunday school programs have dwindled or ended.

3. Don't be surprised if you experience an initial drop off in numbers. Some people won't have the patience or interest in being part of change or an experiment. Many will come back once the kinks are worked out, or once they see that it "works."

4. Make a commitment to this journey for several years. Evaluate and make small adjustments as you move along, but don't make any major changes to your approach for at least two years.

We are in rapidly evolving times, and it is mission critical that we empower one another to face this truth head on. The future of our faith is hanging in the balance. Our faith is asking us to move into a space of not knowing. An evolution of faith formation is the faithful response. We may not be able to fully imagine or visualize the future of faith formation. We may be confronted with experiments that do not go as planned. It is okay to experiment and not succeed. Our power of expertise is gone. Commitment, courage, and the ingenuity of the congregation are all needed now, during the spiritual moment of our time.

> We are searching for new words and new thoughts. Indeed, we stand aquiver on the threshold of a new day; none sees clearly what is in the distance beyond our present experience. The possibilities are as yet untried. But there is a thrill and a glowing hope in being part of a young movement, even though it be small and may long be unpopular.[32]

Ending Sunday school is not tantamount to ending faith formation. To the contrary, faith formation is a foundational ethos of Unitarian Universalist ministries. Paying attention to the shifting needs of our families and children, releasing ourselves from the rigid structures of our past, and boldly experimenting to contribute to the evolution of faith formation may just be the spiritual task of our time. The future of faith formation in New England depends on it. It will be a whole lot easier if we face it together.

Benediction

In the words of Sophia Lyon Fahs:

"Let us all worship together. Let us venture together into the future of faith, determined to keep faith alive because our humanity is only complete when our believing selves are strong and healthy."[33]

"A Power at Work in the Universe"[34] by Tom Schade

My friends,
There is a power at work in the universe.
It works through human hands,
but it was not made by human hands.
It is a creative, sustaining, and transforming power
and we can trust that power with our lives
[and with our ministries].
It will sustain us whenever we take a stand on the side of love; whenever we take a stand for peace and justice;
whenever we take a risk.

Trust in that power.
We are, together, held by that power.

Sources

The Death of Sunday School

[1] "Blue Laws in New England," *Ancestry.com*, accessed May 24, 2017, https://www.ancestry.com/contextux/historicalinsights/new-england-blue-laws.

[2] Christopher L. Walton, "Sophia Lyon Fahs, Revolutionary Educator," *UU World Magazine*, March/April 2003, http://www.uuworld.org/articles/sophia-lyon-fahs-revolutionary-educator.

[3] Tim Wright, "Sunday Schooling Our Kids out of Church," *Patheos*, August 5, 2014, http://sixseeds.patheos.com/timwright/2014/08/sunday-schooling-our-kids-out-of-church.

[4] In families and communities of color, the church has generally played a much more significant role as compared with the dominant white culture in the United States

[5] John Roberto and Katie Pfiffner, "Best Practices in Children's Faith Formation," *Lifelong Faith* 1.3 (2007): http://www.lifelongfaith.com/uploads/5/1/6/4/5164069/lifelong_faith_journal_1.3.pdf.

[6] Mike Allen and Renee Allen, "Generational Differences Chart," accessed May 24, 2017, http://www.wmfc.org/uploads/GenerationalDifferences-Chart.pdf.

[7] John Roberto, "Best Practices in Family Faith Formation," *Lifelong Faith* 1.3 (2007): 21–35, http://www.lifelongfaith.com/uploads/5/1/6/4/5164069/lifelong_faith_journal_1.3.pdf.

[8] Joseph V. Crockett, *Teaching and Learning in American Congregations* (Hartford, CT: Hartford Institute for Religion Research, 2016), http://www.faithcommunitiestoday.org/sites/default/files/Teaching_and_Learning_in_American_Congregations_0.pdf.

[9] Overall, by a 2:1 ratio (51 percent), clergy, rabbis, imams, and priests outnumber all other categories of the "organizers" of congregational teaching and learning ministries. The next largest group is lay volunteers (22 percent). Together, more than 70 percent of congregational educational leaders either have multiple congregational responsibilities or, as lay volunteers, may not have had professional training in religious education. Crockett, *Teaching and Learning in American Congregation*

[10] Gretchen M. Grosky, "The Changing Face of NH: What It Means to Have the 2nd Oldest Population in the Nation," *New Hampshire Union Leader*, August 13, 2016, http://www.unionleader.com/The-changing-face-of- NH:-What-it-means-to-have-the-2nd-oldest-population-in-the-nation.

[11] Art Woolf, "Number of VT Births Lowest since before Civil War," *Burlington Free Press*, June 23, 2016, http://www.burlingtonfreepress.com/story/news/2016/06/23/number-vt-births-lowest-since-before-civil- war/86204456.

[12] Daniel Barrick, *School Consolidation in New Hampshire* (Concord, NH: New Hampshire Center for Public Policy Studies, 2015), http://www.nhpolicy.org/UploadedFiles/Reports/school_consol_forweb.pdf.

[13] While uncommon in New England, there are a small number of congregations reporting growing religious education programs that use a Sunday school model. These are rare exceptions to the rule and are not representative of the majority of experiences reported by New England UU congregations of all sizes.

40

[14] John Roberto, *Faith Formation 2020: Designing the Future of Faith Formation* (Naugatuck, CT: LifelongFaith Associates, 2010).

[15] Edith F. Hunter, *Sophia Lyon Fahs: A Biography* (Boston: Beacon Press, 1966).

[16] Richard Higgins, "Three in a Thousand Identify as Unitarians," *UU World Magazine*, June 2, 2008, http://www.uuworld.org/articles/three-in-thousand-identify-as-unitarians.

[17] Diana Butler Bass, *Process Not Program: Adult Faith Formation for Vital Congregations* (Indianapolis, IN: Congregational Resource Guide, 2010.

The Future of Faith Formation

[18] Paul Rasor, "Can Unitarian Universalism Change?" *UU World Magazine*, February 22, 2010, http://www.uuworld.org/articles/can-uu-change.

[19] Stephanie Martin, "THIS Is Family Ministry: The Experts Speak," *Children's Ministry Magazine*, November 3, 2016, http://childrensministry.com/articles/this-is-family-ministry.

[20] "Tapestry of Faith Curricula," *Unitarian Universalist Association*, accessed May 24, 2017, http://www.uua.org/re/tapestry.

[21] Karen Bellavance-Grace, *Full Week Faith: Rethinking Religious Education and Faith Formation Ministries for Twenty-First Century Unitarian Universalists* (Chicago: The Fahs Collaborative, 2013), http://fullweekfaith.weebly.com/uploads/1/2/2/9/12293877/finalto_web.fahs_fellowship_paper_copy.pdf.

[22] Martin, "THIS Is Family Ministry: The Experts Speak." *Children's Ministry Magazine*. November 3, 2016. http://childrensministry.com/articles/this-is-family- ministry.

[23] The Commission on Appraisal of the Unitarian Universalist Association, *Engaging Our Theological Diversity* (Boston: Unitarian Universalist Association, 2005), http://www.uua.org/sites/live- new.uua.org/files/documents/coa/engagingourtheodiversity.pdf.

[24] Slightly adapted from Thalia Kehoe Rowden, "12 Reasons to Welcome Kids in Church + Tips for Actually Doing It," *Sacraparental,* June 11, 2016, http://sacraparental.com/2016/06/11/12-reasons-welcome-kids- church-tips-actually.

[25] Kara Powell, Brad Griffin, and Cheryl Crawford, "The Church Sticking Together," *Sticky Faith*, October 17, 2011, http://stickyfaith.org/articles/the-church-sticking-together.

[26] Eugene C. Roehlkepartain, *Building Assets, Strengthening Faith: An Intergenerational Survey for Congregations*

[27] Robert Wuthnow, *Growing up Religious: Christians and Jews and Their Journeys of Faith* (Boston: Beacon Press, 2000).

What Have We Learned?

[28] Karen Bauman et al., *LREDA/UUMA/UUMN Task Force for Excellence in Shared Ministry: Preliminary Report* (Huntington Beach, CA: Liberal Religious Educators Association, 2013), http://www.lreda.org/assets/docs/excellence-in-shared-ministry-report.pdf.

[29] Juana Bordas, *Salsa, Soul, and Spirit: Leadership for a Multicultural Age*, 2nd ed. (San Francisco: Berrett- Koehler, 2012).

[30] Ibid.

[31] Gilbert R. Rendle, *Doing the Math of Mission: Fruits, Faithfulness, and Metrics* (Lanham, MD: Rowman & *Littlefield, 2014)*.

[32] Sophia Lyon Fahs, *It Matters What We Believe* (Boston: Beacon Press, 1952).

[33] Sophia Lyon Fahs, Today's Children and Yesterday's Heritage: A Philosophy of Creative Religious Development (Boston: Beacon Press, 1967).

[34] Tom Schade, "A Power at Work in the Universe," *Unitarian Universalist Association*, accessed May 24, 2017, http://www.uua.org/worship/words/benediction/power-at-work.

APPENDICES

Appendix A

Impacts of a Family Ministry Focus on Current Roles

How might focusing on family ministry impact a congregation's...

Governing Board	Devote time and attention to missional conversations. Integrate spiritual practice and reflection into board work as a part of faith formation.
Minister	Engage in truly collaborative shared ministry with Director of Family Ministry, to develop goals, strategies, and resources for meeting the spiritual needs of congregants at every age and stage of spiritual development.
Director of Religious Education	Become a Director of Family Ministry, developing strategies to meet the faith formation needs of people of all ages and at every stage of spiritual development, recognizing that unchurched adults or adults coming from other faith traditions will need as much if not more orientation to Unitarian Universalism as children and youth.
Music Director	Prepare for additional choir members or musicians available to contribute to music ministry as children and teachers are in worship each week and are available to participate.

Membership Professional	Welcoming visitors and guests will no longer necessitate separating families at the door; they will be encouraged to explore the congregation and participate together.
Administrator	May have more space requests on Sunday mornings. Solicit family friendly resources and articles for the newsletter.
Worship Committee	Assess the physical space of worship more regularly (e.g., whether to include rocking chairs at the back of the sanctuary for adults rocking children or for worshippers who need to move, or "pray space"[35] for children and toddlers.) Prepare for a wider cross section of people who can participate in the roles of worship.
Religious Education Committee	Become the Family Ministry Team. May include representatives from other congregational committees to ensure that families are considered when planning for social justice activities, stewardship, small group ministry, etc.
Children and Youth	Welcome into whole congregation worship; offer ways in which to participate through greeting, ushering, readings, music, and even worship planning. Opportunities for age-based gathering may happen before or after Sunday morning worship.

Parents	Able to experience and model worshipping with their children. Able to have opportunities to attend to their own faith formation needs while their children are experiencing age-based gatherings before or after Sunday morning worship (e.g., classes in UU theology, UU identity, small group ministry for parents, mentoring, etc.).
Other Adults	Able to have a variety of opportunities to learn, share, and grow in their own faith formation. May lead or attend classes and conversations after worship. May be more inclined to minister to children and youth without having to sacrifice worshipping on Sunday morning.
Entire Congregation	Able to know and be known by members of all ages. Will exercise patience, understanding, and empathy as they grow into one single congregation. Increased recognition that each person plays a role as both teacher and student, and that we all impact one another's faith formation.

Appendix B

Sample Job Description for Coordinator of Family Ministry (part time)

Summary of Position

The Coordinator of Family Ministry works to ensure that family members are provided with opportunities to grow in their relationship to Unitarian Universalism and respond to that relationship faithfully in the church and the wider world. Primarily an administrative role, the coordinator will work independently on clearly defined tasks, as well as working closely with ministerial and lay leadership.

Spiritual Gifts and Qualifications

- Strong interpersonal relationship skills, with the ability to relate to and motivate people of all ages and backgrounds

- Leadership skills, including the ability to recruit and nurture volunteers and delegate tasks

- Strong verbal and written communication skills, with the ability to speak comfortably before a congregation or other large groups

- Proven commitment to being a positive role model and witness of the Unitarian Universalist faith

- Strong organizational and administrative skills with interest in expanding own knowledge, skills, and abilities

Responsibilities

- Recruit and support volunteers (often with assistance from others)

- Communicate with families

47

- Provide tools for parents and caregivers that equip them in their role as primary spiritual caregivers of their children

- Coordinate the involvement of committees and teams that participate in supporting youth and family activities

- Seek to invite worship visitors, new members, or members not engaged in youth and family ministries to specific events

(Adapted from the Messiah Lutheran Church in Springfield, Missouri)

Appendix C

Sample Job Description for Director of Family Ministry

Summary of Position

The Director of Family Ministry develops and nurtures a ministry for all types of families, striving to guide, nurture, and support all people as they grow in the Unitarian Universalist faith. The Director must pay attention to family circumstance, understand the home as a setting for spiritual formation, and provide relevant and intentional ministry for people of all ages through the church and in the community. All ministry must address basic human needs as well as provide opportunities for faith formation, service, and witness. The Director will work to provide family members with opportunities to grow in their relationship to Unitarian Universalism and respond to that relationship faithfully in the church and the wider world.

Spiritual Gifts and Qualifications

- One or more of these spiritual gifts: teaching, encouragement, leadership, administration, helping, and/or companioning

- Prior leadership experience

- Strong communication skills, including the ability to listen to and communicate with people of all ages

- Ability to work with other ministry leaders, delegate responsibility, and follow up to complete tasks

- Knowledge and respect for Unitarian Universalism and its history, principles, and theology

- A passion for family ministry, including genuine interest in responding to the hopes and concerns of all families in the community and affirming all family units (single and multiple people)

Responsibilities

- Maintain a healthy and growing spiritual life and lead other teachers and leaders in doing the same

- Be attentive to the hopes, concerns, and needs of families of all configurations in the community to determine how the congregation might serve them and how they might serve one another as Unitarian Universalists

- Be familiar with the congregation's overall goals and how they are achieved through the congregation's ministry with families

- Encourage extending the goals of the congregation to include all types of families

- Advocate for all kinds of families, educating the congregation and community about the forms of family life in the twenty-first century and providing families with resources for living their faith

- Work with others to plan and carry out ministry with families in a varied and wide- ranging program that includes worship, study, fellowship, service opportunities, and more

- Build networks with community organizations and people to connect the congregation with the surrounding community for a strong program, including looking for new ministry opportunities

- Encourage other congregational ministry leaders to understand and make all ministries applicable and relevant to varying types of family units

(Adapted from the United Methodist Church)

Appendix D

Examples of Roles for Family Ministry Volunteers or Teams

Welcome and Connection: Ensure that new attendees are warmly welcomed and enthusiastically connected with the congregation, from first impression to ongoing connection through family ministry opportunities.

Second-Hour Religious Education Teacher or Workshop Leader: Teach or assist in weekly classes held after Sunday worship and/or facilitate a learning opportunity or series of sessions aligned with the mission of the congregation.

Small Group Ministry Facilitator: Facilitate weekly or monthly lay-led small groups that provide opportunities for deeper relationships and spiritual exploration.

Faith at Home: Equip members to establish spiritual practices, routines, and reminders of our Unitarian Universalist faith throughout the week.

Events Coordinator: Plan and oversee no more than three family ministry events per year, to occur outside of Sunday morning. Bonus points if they get on the calendar six months in advance.

Sports Outreach: Mobilize members to connect with children and adults in the surrounding community through sports, fitness, and recreational activities, providing opportunities to mentor youth, promote wellness, and engage with people who do not know about Unitarian Universalism.

<u>Mobilization:</u> Motivate and equip members to engage their passions and gifts through volunteer ministry—serving within the church and in the wider community as an expression of the UU faith.

DISCUSSION GUIDE

Session 1:
The Death of Sunday School

Materials

Chalice, candle and lighter or LED battery-operated candle
Newsprint, markers, and tape or handouts
Paper and pens for participants

Preparation

Proposed Agreements (written on newsprint or in hand-outs)

Regarding the *spirit* of our speaking and listening

- We will speak for ourselves and allow others to speak for themselves, with no pressure to represent or explain a whole group.

- We will not criticize the views of others or attempt to persuade them.

- We will listen with resilience, "hanging in" when we hear something that is hard to hear.

Regarding the *form* of our speaking and listening

- We will participate within the time frames suggested by the facilitator and share airtime.

- We will not interrupt except to indicate that we cannot hear a speaker.

- We will "pass" or "pass for now" if we are not ready or willing to respond to a question.

Regarding *confidentiality*

- When we discuss our experience here with people outside the group, we will not attach names or any other identifying information to particular comments unless we have permission to do so.

Chalice Lighting/Opening Reading (3 minutes)

Light the chalice and share these words By Audette Fulbright Fulson

This light we kindle
is set in the lamp of our history.
We inherit this free faith
from the brave and gentle, fierce and outspoken
hearts and minds that have come before us.
Let us be worthy inheritors of this faith
and through our good works, pass it boldly to a new generation.

Agreements (10 minutes)

PURPOSES - To help the group craft a set of communication agreements that will serve the purposes of the dialogue and that everyone understands and agrees to observe.

Say something like... I have a draft set of proposed communication agreements that are often helpful in creating a respectful environment for speaking and listening. Your handout (or a posted sheet) lists some guidelines often used to create an environment where people can speak openly and listen fully. Please take a moment to read them, and then I'll check in with you to see if you'd like to adopt them as-is or revise them for our group.

After reading the proposed agreements, say something like... Are there questions about what any of these proposed agreements mean? Would you like to suggest revisions or additions.

If suggestions are made and agreed to by all, add them to the list. Is each of you willing to observe these agreements as best you can and to authorize me to remind you if you forget?

Make sure you see or hear a verbal or nonverbal signal of commitment from each participant before moving on. OK, these will serve as our agreements. If at any point you feel that these agreements are not adequately serving your purposes, speak up and we'll see if as a group you would like to revise them.

Introductions and First Impressions (15 minutes)

Tell the group you will invite each person to introduce themselves and take a sentence or two to speak of one idea, impression, or question that was provoked by reading the paper. Allow silence for two or three

56

minutes for people to find their words. Then, invite each person in turn to speak briefly uninterrupted, asking them to limit their thoughts to a point or two. Mention that for this conversation and any others, each person reserves the right to pass. If your group has more than six participants, consider dividing into groups of three or four to share impressions.

Sharing (30 minutes)

Invite participants to share, one at a time, without interruption stories about their own faith journey, responding as they wish to one or more of these questions:

> What thoughts and feelings are you sitting with as you reflect back on The Death of Sunday School and the Future of Faith Formation? Can you say something about your personal or professional experiences that may relate to your having those thoughts and feelings?
>
> What pieces of information—or ways of looking at information—were new to you?
>
> What insights did you gain from this paper?

Responding (20 Minutes)

" Sunday schools were originally places where poor children could learn to read. Sunday schools were designed as an outreach mission to take neglected, unsupervised and poorly behaved children of the streets."

To your mind, what are Sunday schools designed for today?

Conversation (10 minutes)

Invite participants to respond to what other have shared. Remind them that the group has covenanted to speak from personal experience and perspectives, rather than challenging the validity of another's experiences and perspectives.

Closing Reading (2 minutes)

"A Power at Work in the Universe" by Tom Schade

My friends,
There is a power at work in the universe.
It works through human hands,
but it was not made by human hands.
It is a creative, sustaining, and transforming power
and we can trust that power with our lives
[and with our ministries].
It will sustain us whenever we take a stand on the side of love; whenever we take a stand for peace and justice;
whenever we take a risk.

Trust in that power.
We are, together, held by that power.

Session 2:

The Future of Faith Formation

Materials

Chalice, candle and lighter or LED battery-operated candle
Newsprint, markers, and tape or handouts
Paper and pens for participants

Preparation

Proposed Agreements (written on newsprint or in handouts)

Regarding the *spirit* of our speaking and listening

- We will speak for ourselves and allow others to speak for themselves, with no pressure to represent or explain a whole group.

- We will not criticize the views of others or attempt to persuade them.

- We will listen with resilience, "hanging in" when we hear something that is hard to hear.

Regarding the *form* of our speaking and listening

- We will participate within the time frames suggested by the facilitator and share airtime.

- We will not interrupt except to indicate that we cannot hear a speaker.

- We will "pass" or "pass for now" if we are not ready or willing to respond to a question.

Regarding *confidentiality*

- When we discuss our experience here with people outside the group, we will not attach names or any other identifying information to particular comments unless we have permission to do so.

Chalice Lighting/Opening Reading (3 minutes)

Light the chalice and share these words By Robin F. Gray

By the light of this chalice
we prepare for the future.
We prepare ourselves
for the times of triumph
and times of trial that might come. We prepare ourselves to be present
to one another with loving hearts even in the most difficult of times.
We prepare ourselves

to make the connections
that will lift us out of isolation
and prepare the path of justice and equality.

Agreements (10 minutes)

PURPOSES - To help the group craft a set of communication agreements that will serve the purposes of the dialogue and that everyone understands and agrees to observe.

Say something like... I have a draft set of proposed communication agreements that are often helpful in creating a respectful environment for speaking and listening. Your handout (or a posted sheet) lists some guidelines often used to create an environment where people can speak openly and listen fully. Please take a moment to read them, and then I'll check in with you to see if you'd like to adopt them as-is or revise them for our group.

After reading the proposed agreements, say something like... Are there questions about what any of these proposed agreements mean? Would you like to suggest revisions or additions.

If suggestions are made and agreed to by all, add them to the list. Is each of you willing to observe these agreements as best you can and to authorize me to remind you if you forget?

Make sure you see or hear a verbal or nonverbal signal of commitment from each participant before moving on. OK, these will serve as our agreements. If at any point you feel that these agreements are not adequately serving your purposes, speak up and we'll see if as a group you would like to revise them.

Introductions and First Impressions (25 minutes)

Tell the group you will invite each person to introduce themselves and take a sentence or two to speak of one idea, impression, or question that was provoked by reading the paper. Allow silence for two or three minutes for people to find their words. Then, invite each person in turn to speak briefly uninterrupted, asking them to limit their thoughts to a point or two. Mention that for this conversation and any others, each person reserves the right to pass. If your group has more than six participants, consider dividing into groups of three or four to share impressions.

Sharing (35 minutes)

Invite participants to share, one at a time, without interruption stories about their own faith journey, responding as they wish to one or more of these questions:

> Do you have uncertainties about any of the assumptions and views you have held in the past? Can you say something about both the certainties and uncertainties you bring to this conversation?
>
> What are your views, hopes, and fears regarding the future of faith formation? What is the "heart of the matter" for you?
>
> As a committee/staff team/small group/etc, are we willing to explore this further? What do we need from one another to do that?
>
> How can this conversation be continued in our congregation?

Conversation (15 minutes)

Invite participants to respond to what others have shared. Remind them that the group covenanted to speak from personal experience and perspectives, rather than challenging the validity of another's experiences and perspectives.

Closing Reading (2 minutes)
from The 2013 LREDA/UUMA/UUMN Task Force for Excellence in Shared Ministry: Preliminary Report

The best we can hope for our religion is that the future we co-create is rooted in our heretical heritage. We stand on the shoulders of people who, against mandates of their day, promoted counter-cultural ideas. "Freedom, reason, and tolerance," resounded from their lips and their living, though their world was steeped in proscription and intolerance. Still, we must acknowledge that while this is our foundation, it is not our current battle. Tolerance and freedom are touted widely in popular culture. Quests of the individual (See me. Accept me. Make room for me.) fail to address the desperate isolation in which we all live.

Our faith currently offers a vital alternative. Without the dictates of dogma, we are freed to create the substantive covenantal communities in which people can recover a sense of connection to self, others and spirit. Ours is the religion that binds us first to the other and in doing so to all that is holy or life itself. We can hold each other. We can love each other because of who we are not in spite of who we are. We can love each other into being more.

Session 3:

Family Ministry

Materials

Chalice, candle and lighter or LED battery-operated candle
Newsprint, markers, and tape or handouts
Paper and pens for participants

Preparation

Proposed Agreements (written on newsprint or in hand-outs)

Regarding the *spirit* of our speaking and listening

- We will speak for ourselves and allow others to speak for themselves, with no pressure to represent or explain a whole group.

- We will not criticize the views of others or attempt to persuade them.

- We will listen with resilience, "hanging in" when we hear something that is hard to hear.

Regarding the *form* of our speaking and listening

- We will participate within the time frames suggested by the facilitator and share airtime.

- We will not interrupt except to indicate that we cannot hear a speaker.

- We will "pass" or "pass for now" if we are not ready or willing to respond to a question.

Regarding *confidentiality*

- When we discuss our experience here with people outside the group, we will not attach names or any other identifying information to particular comments unless we have permission to do so.

Chalice Lighting/Opening Reading (3 minutes)

Light the chalice and share these words By Kathy A Huff

Spirit of life, be present with us this hour. Join us today as we gather in a wider search for truth and purpose. In this quest, may we greet one another with open hearts and minds; may we inspire each other to consider new questions and seek deeper meaning; and may we cultivate wisdom and compassion. Let all who enter this sanctuary see a welcome face, hear a kind word, and find comfort in this community. And may all that is done and said here today be in service to love and justice.

Agreements (10 minutes)

PURPOSES - T o help the group craft a set of communication agreements that will serve the purposes of the dialogue and that everyone understands and agrees to observe.

Say something like... I have a draft set of proposed communication agreements that are often helpful in creating a respectful environment for speaking and listening. Your handout (or a posted sheet) lists some guidelines often used to create an environment where people can speak openly and listen fully. Please take a moment to read them, and then I'll check in with you to see if you'd like to adopt them as-is or revise them for our group.

After reading the proposed agreements, say something like... Are there questions about what any of these proposed agreements mean? Would you like to suggest revisions or additions.

If suggestions are made and agreed to by all, add them to the list. Is each of you willing to observe these agreements as best you can and to authorize me to remind you if you forget?

Make sure you see or hear a verbal or nonverbal signal of commitment from each participant before moving on. OK, these will serve as our agreements. If at any point you feel that these agreements are not adequately serving your purposes, speak up and we'll see if as a group you would like to revise them.

Introductions and First Impressions (15 minutes)

Tell the group you will invite each person to introduce themselves and take a sentence or two to speak of one idea, impression, or question that was provoked by reading the paper. Allow silence for two or three minutes for people to find their words. Then, invite each person in turn to speak briefly uninterrupted, asking them to limit their thoughts to a point or two. Mention that for this conversation and any others, each person reserves the right to pass. If your group has more than six participants, consider dividing into groups of three or four to share impressions.

Sharing (30 minutes)

Invite participants to share, one at a time, without interruption stories about their own faith journey, responding as they wish to one or more of these questions:

> How has the congregation supported faith formation at both church and home for you and your family?
>
> Share a story of how you have brought your faith out of the sanctuary and into your life.
>
> Who has influenced you to be a spiritual leader for your children or other young people in your

Responding (20 minutes)

Invite participants to share, one at a time and without interruption, their responses or reactions to one of the passages below:

The church realizes it can't be effective alone and needs the home. As family ministry expands, it's also evolving. Just being family-friendly no longer counts. The old approach of keeping people of all ages busy with lots of family-specific programming is missing the mark. All the "random acts of ministry" that churches line up for families overload church and family schedules, ultimately "competing with the very families you're trying to help." (Reggie Joiner, founder and president of the reThink Group)

"Family ministry needs to be about churches intentionally influencing parents to be the spiritual leader for their kids. A child might attend church some fifty hours per year, but a parent or caregiver has more like three thousand hours per year to impact the heart of their child— an influence that is lifelong. As good as we might think we are as a church and as electrifying and relevant as our ministries might be, we still don't have the potential to influence children the way parents do." (Mike Clear, family life pastor at Discovery Church in Simi Valley, California)

Conversation (10 minutes)

Invite participants to respond to what others have shared. Remind them that the group has covenanted to speak from personal experience and perspectives, rather than challenging the validity of another's experiences and perspectives.

Closing Reading (2 minutes)

By Harold E Babcock

And now may we go forth
in the certainty of faith,
in the knowledge of love,
and in the vision of hope.
And in our going, may we be blessed with all good things on this day
and forevermore. Amen.

Congregational Conversations: A Taste of Dialogue

The Death of Sunday School and the Future of Faith Formation

Adapted from Fostering Dialogue Across Divides | whatisessential.org

Welcome and Orientation 5 MINUTES

PURPOSES - To welcome participants and to remind them about the purpose and spirit of the dialogue. To say something about roles, schedule, etc., so people know what to expect.

WELCOME AND RESTATEMENT OF PURPOSE

Welcome participants, introduce yourself, and say something like... Welcome. Before I invite you to introduce yourselves, I'd like to say a few words about dialogue. I also want to orient you to the plan for the evening and what you can expect from me and from one another.

As you probably know, dialogue is different from debate; in fact dialogue can sometimes serve as an antidote to the divisiveness that often occurs when debates get stuck in ruts. Debates can be clarifying and educational but they can also be over-simplifying and polarizing. They often reduce people's views and commitments to slogans and simplistic assertions. I expect that slogans and labels rarely do justice to the variety of perspectives that people have, or to the complexity of people's thoughts and feelings, yours included.

Tonight you'll have an opportunity to say something about your own views or response to The Death of Sunday School and how they've been shaped by your life experiences. And you'll be invited to say what you feel clear about, what you find confusing, what you feel conflicted about, and to learn more about the views of others.

So this is an opportunity to have an exchange that is focused not on debating or persuading, but on better understanding other people's views and being better understood by others. This dialogue may even help you understand your own views better. The plan for tonight may feel a bit too structured at times, but we've found that some structure at the beginning can help people to speak and listen in ways that foster mutual understanding.

SCHEDULE AND ENDING TIME

Say something like... Let me tell you a little bit about the how of the dialogue.

We'll begin by making some *communication agreements* for our time together.

Then we'll have a quick go-round in which you can briefly *introduce yourselves.*

Next we'll have three go-rounds in which you can respond to questions that I will pose.

Following the go-rounds, we'll have some time for *less-structured conversation* in which you can explore connections among your experiences

70

and perspectives. Those connections might take the form of one person asking another person a question. Or they might take the form of simply noting similarities and differences and exploring them a bit further.

We'll take time at the end for each of you to say some *parting words* about the dialogue.

Finally we will ask you to give us brief *written feedback*.

Our *ending time* is [time]. Can everyone stay until then?

Tip: I f people have to leave early, find out how they will leave (e.g., by saying a few parting words or by just getting up to leave quietly) and determine how you will get their feedback.

PENS AND PAPER

Say something like... I have provided pens and paper so you can make notes for yourself as we go along. This can help you to organize your thoughts while you're preparing to answer a question and give you a place to store thoughts and questions that come up while you are listening to others. You also can note interesting themes, differences, and convergences to bring up during the less-structured part of your time together.

YOUR ROLE

Say something like... In my role as facilitator, I will guide you through the dialogue and ensure that you either follow or renegotiate whatever communications agreements you make with each other. I'll also keep track of time. If I've asked you to speak for no more than three minutes and you've gone over that time, I'll signal you by [indicate how],

71

to ask you to complete your thought. You don't need to stop mid-sentence.

Do you have any questions about my role as facilitator? If at any point you have concerns about how things are going, or how I'm playing my role, please let me know and we will find a way to address those concerns together. Can I count on that?

Agreements 10 MINUTES

PURPOSES - To help the group craft a set of communication agreements that will serve the purposes of the dialogue and that everyone understands and agrees to observe.

Say something like... I have a draft set of proposed communication agreements that are often helpful in creating a respectful environment for speaking and listening. Your handout (or a posted sheet) lists some guidelines often used to create an environment where people can speak openly and listen fully. Please take a moment to read them, and then I'll check in with you to see if you'd like to adopt them as-is or revise them for our group.

PROPOSED AGREEMENTS

Regarding the spirit of our speaking and listening:

1. We will speak for ourselves and allow others to speak for themselves and with no pressure to represent or explain a whole group.

2. We will not criticize the views of others or attempt to persuade them.

3. We will listen with resilience, "hanging in" when we hear something that is hard to hear.

Regarding the form of our speaking and listening:

1. We will participate within the time frames suggested by the facilitator and share "airtime."

2. We will not interrupt except to indicate that we cannot hear a speaker.

3. We will "pass" or "pass for now" if we are not ready or willing to respond to a question.

Regarding confidentiality:

1. When we discuss our experience here with people outside the group, we will not attach names or any other identifying information to particular comments unless we have permission to do so.

After reading the proposed agreements, say something like... Are there questions about what any of these proposed agreements mean? Would you like to suggest revisions or additions.

If suggestions are made and agreed to by all, add them to the list. I s each of you willing to observe these agreements as best you can and to authorize me to remind you if you forget?

Make sure you see or hear a verbal or nonverbal signal of commitment from each participant before moving on. OK, these will serve as our agreements. If at any point you feel that these agreements are not adequately serving your purposes, speak up and we'll see if as a group you would like to revise them.

Introductions and Hopes 15 MINUTES

PURPOSES - To give participants an opportunity to say something about themselves and/or share their hopes for the dialogue.

Decide on the instructions you will use and say something like... Let's start by going around and saying your name and...

Choose one of these: Something you had to leave behind to be here tonight (for example, a task undone, a baseball game, a child wanting help with a science project). OR Something about yourself that you'd like other people to know, which doesn't relate to [the topic]. It could be about work, play, passions, or pre-occupations —anything.

AND choose one of these: Something that led you to accept the invitation to join this dialogue. OR Something that you hope to experience or learn while you are here.

Specify a time frame. It's often difficult to answer questions like these briefly because there's so much you could say, so please take a minute to choose just a few things to tell us. When we go around I'll ask you to speak for no more than two minutes each.

After a minute of silent reflection, repeat the questions and say something like...

Any one of you can start when you are ready. Then we'll go around the circle clockwise from that point. If we come to you before you are ready, you can pass and I'll check in with you later to see if you'd like to speak then. I'll signal you if two minutes has passed.

First Question (A TWO-PART QUESTION) 20 MINUTES 3 MINUTES PER PERSON

PURPOSES - To invite participants to connect their views with their life experiences.

Choose the first question and say something like... Now I invite you to take up to three minutes to respond to the following question(s):

1. Please share a life experience that might help others understand how you came to have the perspectives, concerns or values you have related to faith formation. First, let's take a minute so you can collect your thoughts.

After a minute to reflect, repeat the question and remind the participants about the time frame.

Any one of you can start when you are ready. Then we'll go around the circle clockwise from that point. If we come to you before you are ready, you can pass and I'll check in with you later to see if you'd like to speak then. I'll signal you if three minutes has passed.

Second Question 15 MINUTES 2 MINUTES PER PERSON

PURPOSES - To encourage participants to articulate the core of their perspective— the values, hopes, fears, and assumptions at the center of their convictions.

Say something like... Again, I'd like to pose a question and, this time, ask you to take up to two minutes to respond. Here's the question:

2. What is at the heart of the matter for you? (In other words, what is it that really matters to you related to faith formation and the death of Sunday school?) First, take a minute to collect your thoughts.

After a minute of reflection, repeat the question and, as before, say something like... Any one of you can start when you are ready. Then we'll go around the circle clockwise from that point. If we come to you before you are ready, you can pass and I'll check in with you later to see if you'd like to speak then. I'll signal you if two minutes has passed.

Tip: I f people are focusing more on the specifics of their views and less on what's at the core or heart of the matter you can ask, "In what you've said, what do you think is at the heart of the matter for you?" Or, "What core values or fears or hopes shape your way of looking at the issues?

Third Question 20 MINUTES 3 MINUTES PER PERSON

PURPOSES - To encourage participants to reflect on and share some of the complexities of their views.

Say something like... Again, I'd like to pose a question. This is a complicated one, so I'll give you plenty of time to think about it. Then you'll each have up to three minutes to respond.

Pose a question that asks participants to speak about their uncertainties, gray areas, or value conflicts related to the issue, for example [choose one]... Within your overall perspective on faith formation and Sunday school are there areas of uncertainty or a value conflict that you're willing to *speak about? For example On the one hand I really care about meeting the needs of our families and on the other hand I care about or appreciate our Sunday school program so it's a little complicated for me.*

That's a lot to take in so I'll repeat the question and ask that you let me know if you don't understand it.

Repeat the question slowly. Let's take a minute to reflect on this before anyone speaks.

After a minute, repeat the questions and add... We'll start with whoever is ready, then we'll go around. If your turn comes before you are ready, you can pass and I'll check in with you later to see if you'd like to speak then.

Tip: I f participants already have spoken about their uncertainties and value conflicts, you can acknowledge that and invite them to say more about their views, worries, or hopes.

Questions of Curiosity 25 MINUTES
PURPOSES - To foster a more organic conversation that deepens understanding of what has been heard and explores connections among the participants' views and experiences.

Say something like... We are now at the point in our time together when you can talk more freely. As the structure of the conversation loosens, it's important to remember why you are here: not to debate or persuade, but to understand.

Introduce the four pathways to connected conversation either briefly as follows or with a handout.

At this point you can ask questions, identify and pursue a theme, explore similarities and differences, or comment on how something you've heard has been enriching or, perhaps, unsettling.

PATHWAYS TO A CONNECTED CONVERSATION

Note a point of learning - Have you heard something that stirred fresh thoughts or feelings?

77

Pick up and weave a thread - Has an interesting theme or idea emerged that you'd like to add to?

Clarify differences - Have you heard an apparent difference that disturbed you in some way? If so, first check to see if you understood it correctly. Then you might say what was disturbing and why. Or you might ask a question that is likely to surface the values or assumptions that underlie the difference.

Ask a question - Is there something someone said that you'd like to understand better? If you ask a question, be sure it reflects genuine curiosity and is not a challenge in disguise.

Invite questions first - Let's take a minute to think, then let's start by hearing what questions you have for each other.

After allowing a minute or so for participants to reflect in silence say something like... I s there anyone who would like to ask a question?

After questions, open up the other pathways to connected conversations.

Parting Words 15 MINUTES

PURPOSES - To encourage participants to reflect on what they have learned or valued. To invite participants to say something that will bring their participation to a satisfying close.

Say something like... Our time here is coming to an end. Are there any parting words that you'd like to say to bring your participation to a close? You may want to simply comment on what the experience has been like for you. Or you may want to mention one idea, feeling, commitment, or question that you are taking with you, or something

78

about what came up for you here that you may want to share with a friend, family member, or congregant.

After hearing from all who wish to speak, thank the participants, and ask them to fill out feedback forms. Say who will see the forms and how they will be used.

A Sample Set of Proposed Agreements

Adapted from Fostering Dialogue Across Divides | <u>whatisessential.org</u>

1. *We will speak for ourselves.* W e will not try to represent a whole group, and we will not ask others to represent, defend, or explain an entire group.

2. *We will avoid making grand pronouncements* and, instead, connect what we know and believe to our experiences, in influences in our lives, particular sources of information, etc.

3. *We will refrain from characterizing the views of others in a critical spirit,* keeping in mind that we are here to understand each other, not to persuade each other.

4. *We will listen with resilience,* " hanging in" when we hear something that is hard to hear.

5. *We will share airtime and refrain from interrupting others.*

6. *We will "pass" or "pass for now"* i f we are not ready or willing to respond to a question—no explanation required.·

7. *If asked to keep something confidential, we will honor the request.* In conversations outside of the group we will not attribute partic-

80

ular statements to particular individuals by name or identifying information without permission.

8. *We will avoid making negative attributions* a bout the beliefs, values, and motives of other participants, e.g., "You only say that because...". When tempted to do so, we will consider the possibility of testing the assumption we are making by asking a question, e.g., "Why is that important to you?"

9. *We will use email only for scheduling,* not for substantive discussion.

Proposed Agreements

Adapted from Fostering Dialogue Across Divides | whatisessential.org

Regarding the *spirit* of our speaking and listening

1. We will speak for ourselves and allow others to speak for themselves, with no pressure to represent or explain a whole group.

2. We will not criticize the views of others or attempt to persuade them.

3. We will listen with resilience, "hanging in" when we hear something that is hard to hear.

Regarding the *form* of our speaking and listening

1. We will participate within the time frames suggested by the facilitator and share airtime.

2. We will not interrupt except to indicate that we cannot hear a speaker.

3. We will "pass" or "pass for now" if we are not ready or willing to respond to a question.

Regarding *confidentiality*

1. When we discuss our experience here with people outside the group, we will not attach names or any other identifying information to particular comments unless we have permission to do so.

Four Pathways to a Connected Conversation

Adapted from Fostering Dialogue Across Divides | whatisessential.org

Note a point of learning - Have you heard something that stirred fresh thoughts or feelings?

Pick up and weave a thread - Has an interesting theme or idea emerged that you'd like to add to?

Clarify differences - Have you heard an apparent difference that disturbed you in some way? If so, first check to see if you understood it correctly. Then you might say what was disturbing and why. Or you might ask a question that is likely to surface the values or assumptions that underlie the difference.

Ask a question - I s there something someone said that you'd like to understand better? If you ask a question, be sure it reflects genuine curiosity and is not a challenge in disguise.

Congregational Conversations: A Taste of Dialogue (handout)

The Death of Sunday School and the Future of Faith Formation

Adapted from Fostering Dialogue Across Divides | whatisessential.org

Agreements:

We will speak for ourselves and allow others to speak for themselves and with no pressure to represent or explain a whole group.

We will participate within the time frames suggested by the facilitator and share "airtime."

We will not interrupt except to indicate that we cannot hear a speaker.

We will "pass" or "pass for now" if we are not ready or willing to respond to a question.

When we discuss our experience here with people outside the group, we will not attach names or any other identifying information to particular comments unless we have permission to do so.

Structured Go-Rounds:

One person read the question aloud. One person times two minutes of silent reflection to prepare to speak.

The first person speaks for two minutes and then each person follows, going clockwise. You can always "pass" or "pass for now" without explanation.

Pause between speakers so that what was spoken can be fully heard and absorbed.

Time each other, passing the timer at the end of two minutes, to indicate the speaker's time has ended.

As you listen to others, make notes about things you'd like to learn more about. You will have the opportunity to ask questions of each other next.

Question One (Up to two minutes each)

Please share a life experience that might help others understand how you came to have the perspectives, concerns or values you have related to faith formation.

Question Two (Up to two minutes each)

What is at the heart of the matter for you? (In other words, what is it that really matters to you related to these issues?)

Question Three (Up to two minutes each)

As you think about your perspectives and experiences with this issue, can you speak about any ways you might be pulled in different directions? Like: On the one hand I really care about meeting the needs of our families and on the other hand I care about or appreciate our Sunday school program so it's a little complicated for me.

Questions of Curiosity (25 minutes total)

Now is the time to pose questions to each other, preferably ones that spring from your curiosity and desire to better understand the speaker.

Parting Words (Up to one minutes each)

What would you like to continue thinking or dialoguing about?

Self-Help Tools for Participants

Adapted from Fostering Dialogue Across Divides | <u>whatisessential.org</u>

If you feel cut off , say so or override the interruption. ("I'd like to finish...")

If you feel misunderstood, clarify what you mean. ("Let me put this another way...")

If you feel misheard, ask the listener to repeat what she heard you say and a rm or correct her statement.

If you feel hurt or disrespected, say so. If possible, describe exactly what you heard or saw that evoked hurt feelings in you. ("When you said x, I felt y..." where "x" refers to specific language.) If it is hard to think of what to say, just say "OUCH" to flag your reaction.

If you feel angry, express the anger directly ("I felt angry when I heard you say x...") rather than expressing it or acting it out indirectly (by trashing another person's statement or asking a sarcastic or rhetorical question).

If you feel confused , frame a question that seeks clarification or more information. You may prefer to paraphrase what you have heard. ("Are you saying that...?")

If you feel uncomfortable with the process , state your discomfort and check in with the group to see how others are experiencing what is happening. ("I'm not comfortable with the tension I'm feeling in the room right now, and I'm wondering how others are feeling.") If others share your concerns and you have an idea about what would

87

help, offer that idea. ("How about taking a one-minute Time Out to reflect on what we are trying to do together?")

If you feel the conversation is going off track , share your perception, and check in with others. ("I thought we were going to discuss x before moving to y, but it seems that w bypassed x and are focusing on y.)

Participant Feedback Form

Adapted from Fostering Dialogue Across Divides | <u>whatisessential.org</u>

1. What was most satisfying, enriching, or valuable about your experience in this dialogue?

2. What was less than satisfying, frustrating, or disappointing?

3. Can you say something about what you are taking away from the experience?

4. What advice or suggestions can you offer to people designing future dialogues on this issue?

5. Other comments?

6. Name?

SMALL GROUP MINISTRY

Small Group Ministry Session

The History of Sunday School: Where Have We Come From?

Opening Words: Saved by Hope, by Faith, by Love

By <u>Reinhold Neibuhr</u>

"Nothing that is worth doing can be achieved in our lifetime; therefore we must be saved by hope. Nothing which is true or beautiful or good makes complete sense in any immediate context of history; therefore we must be saved by faith. Nothing we do, however virtuous, can be accomplished alone; therefore we are saved by love."

Check-in

Focus/Topic:

Sunday schools were originally designed as an outreach mission created to take neglected, unsupervised and poorly behaved children off the streets. The Bible was the textbook used to teach these children how to read. Over the course of a century and a half Sunday school evolved from an educational and missionary venture, into a cornerstone of towns and neighborhoods in the US. Attending Sunday school was the cultural norm.

The Sunday school model we recognize today came to life in the 1940's and 50's. Church and religion still played a significant role in US culture. Sunday school classes mimicked the structure of public schools, providing age-segregated classes for children to receive religious instruction and lessons.

Today, nearly 70 years later, we can hardly think of a single area of our lives that has not undergone tremendous change. We must ask ourselves if our Sunday school model has evolved and changed with the rest of the world.

Questions...

What role did church play in the life of your family growing up? If you grew up unchurched, what role did you witness church playing in the lives of families around you?

How have you noticed the role of church and religion in society evolve?

Why do we offer Sunday School today? What is it's purpose?

Likes & Wishes

Closing Words: Be About the Work

By Andrea Hawkins-Kamper

May we see all as it is, and may it all be as we see it.

May we be the ones to make it as it should be,

For if not us, who? If not now, when?

This is answering the cry of justice with the work of peace,

This is redeeming the pain of history with the grace of wisdom,

This is the work we are called to do, and this is the call we answer now:

To be the barrier and the bridge,

To be the living embodiment of our Principles,

To be about the work of building the Beloved Community,

To be a people of intention and a people of conscience.

Small Group Ministry Session

Who Are the People in Your Neighborhood?

Opening Words: We Prepare For the Future
By Robin F. Gray

By the light of this chalice

we prepare for the future.

We prepare ourselves

for the times of triumph

and times of trial that might come.

We prepare ourselves to be present

to one another with loving hearts

even in the most difficult of times.

We prepare ourselves

to make the connections

that will lift us out of isolation

and prepare the path of justice and equality.

Check-in

Focus/Topic:

Currently the United States is undergoing a massive shift in demographics. What was once a white protestant nation is now transformed into a cross cultural, multi ethnic and religious landscape. If churches want to meet the challenges of the twenty-first century, then they must be prepared to change to meet the needs of the ever-shifting cultural climate. And to meet those needs of the ever shifting cultural climate, they need to be aware of it first.

At First Baptist Church East Nashville, this predominantly black congregation once mirrored the neighborhood's demographics, but today the hip and eclectic East Nashville with its rising property values and trendy restaurants draws a number of white millennials.

Rev. Morris Tipton Jr., the church's pastor strongly believes that a church should be a part of its community. He said First Baptist Church East Nashville's congregation is healthy and about 75 people fill the pews every Sunday. But he also is trying to reach the people who live next door, both those in the luxury apartments as well as the resident in a Section 8 housing complex behind the church. This congregation had to wrestle with not only the changing identity of who their community was, but how they were gong to engage them.

Questions...

Have changes in our congregation reflected changes in the area?

Who are we called to serve?

Are we called to serve the needs of the neighborhood/community?

What happens when the neighborhood or community changes? How does the church respond to those changes....or does it?

Likes & Wishes

Closing Words: We Meet on Holy Ground

By Richard S. Gilbert

We meet on holy ground,

Brought into being as life encounters life,

As personal histories merge into the communal story,

As we take on the pride and pain of our companions,

As separate selves become community.

How desperate is our need for one another:

Our silent beckoning to our neighbors,

Our invitations to share life and death together,

Our welcome into the lives of those we meet,

And their welcome into our own.

May our souls capture this treasured time.

May our spirits celebrate our meeting

In this time and in this space,

For we meet on holy ground.

Source: "Becoming: A Spiritual Guide for Navigating Adulthood"

Small Group Ministry Session

Modern Family: The Needs of the 21st Century Family

Opening Words:

A vision for Unitarian Universalism in a multicultural world

By UUA Leadership Council

With humility and courage born of our history, we are called as Unitarian Universalists to build the Beloved Community where all souls are welcome as blessings, and the human family lives whole and reconciled. With this vision in our hearts and minds, we light our chalice.

"A vision for Unitarian Universalism in a multicultural world" by the Unitarian Universalist Association (UUA) Leadership Council, adopted October 1, 2008 (adapted as a chalice lighting May 2009)

Check-in

Focus/Topic:

The Surprising Truth a Parent Really Wants to Tell You

By: Christine Yount Jones

I watched you this past Sunday as you were running from room to room—making sure kiddos and volunteers were where they needed to be and that they had the necessary supplies. I saw you smiling as you encountered each child and family. I watched you chase down a runaway toddler.

It makes me think of my own life-juggling act. Though, I'll admit, you're much more graceful. After a day of school drop-off, driving here and there, work, sports and music practice, more driving, homework, and chores, I'm finally sitting down for a quick minute of sanity. A quick breath. That's the key word: quick.

I notice you week after week—always with a smile on your face and in your heart. What time do you arrive on Sunday morning? I wonder. How late do you work after your other full-time job? How do you keep smiling when you're elbow-deep in vomit or tears? I don't know how you do it.

Watching you made me realize I needed to take the time to let you know how I really feel about my child being in your ministry. Here are my honest thoughts—laid bare for you to read.

Mostly, I want my child to be noticed and loved. On Sundays he's up before I am—dressed and ready. He loves coming to church and can't wait to see you, his teacher, and his friends. That's what it's all about—relationships. All the programming in the world can't replace relationships. And I promise I don't mind being "ignored" when we walk up to you. I love that you're focused on him, talk with him, and give him a hug. You make him feel so special when you call him by name. At that moment, he feels like the most important person in the world because you know his name.

I do want to hear from you. I'm a firm believer that raising a child truly does take a village. You, his school teacher, friends, family, and I all play unique roles in his life. I need help, and I want to hear from you. I want to reinforce what he's learning in your ministry and receive tips and dinnertime discussion starters. But, please: Keep it simple. Send a monthly email because you know how papers get lost. It's icing on the cake to hear from you or his teacher when you see him doing something great—asking an intriguing question, helping others, or engaging in a game. You have no idea how positive encouragement keeps me going.

Less is sometimes more, my friend. Brutal honesty here: Our family can't handle more monthly events. I know you're dedicated, have great ideas, and want to give only your best to the children in our church. But honestly, we're tired. Would you consider combining events to cover multiple goals? One family event for the entire family—parents, teenagers, and children—with a service project component can be an effective (and efficient!) way to engage families in community for the sake of others. Take a month off of planning an extra event for our kids. You'll be freed up to focus more deeply on fewer events, and our family can spend more downtime together—a precious and fleeting thing.

Most of all, thank you! Thank you for getting out of bed each Sunday morning—even with a CamelBak full of coffee. Thanks for researching for the interactive, applicable, and effective lessons that kids will enjoy and understand. Thank you for smiling—even when your heart is breaking for a child in your care. Thank you for investing in my child's life. It's an eternal investment that he will never forget. And neither will I.

Sincerely,

A Parent

Questions...

> How has being a member of this church helped you to be a better parent/child/partner/sibling/family member?
>
> What do families need from the church that they can't find anywhere else?
>
> Brene Brown suggests, "We can minimize competitiveness within our faith communities by insisting our churches become "Societies of Imperfect Parents." How might we help parents realize inadequacy is a universal condition and church is a place to give and receive grace?

Likes & Wishes

Closing Words: As We Part Now One From Another

By Eileen B Karpeles

As we part now one from another, let these be our thoughts:

If that which is most holy lies within the human person, and if the greatest power in the world shines flickering and uncertain from each individual heart, then it is easy to see the value of human associations

100

dedicated to nurturing that light: the couple, the family, the religious community.

For the power of good in any one of us must at times waver. But when a group together is dedicated to nurturing the power of good, it is rare for the light to grow dim in all individuals at the same moment.

So we borrow courage and wisdom from one another, to warm us and keep us until we're together again.

Source: 1997 UUMA Worship Materials Collection; altered